GHOS
OF DARTMOOR

SALLY & CHIPS BARBER

TOR MARK

First published as *Dark and Dastardly* by Obelisk Publications, 1988

This 2020 edition published by Tor Mark Ltd,
United Downs Industrial Estate,
Redruth, Cornwall TR16 5HY

www.tormark.co.uk

ISBN 978 0 85025 468 6

Text: © Tor Mark
Images: © Adobe 2020, © Jane Reynolds, page 15 © Andy Brown, page 21 © Martin Brewster,
page 30 © Jeremy Willcocks, © Shutterstock 2020, © Tor Mark
Map: © Tor Mark
Layout: © Tor Mark

Printed and bound in the UK

- CONTENTS -

- INTRODUCTION -

If you stand alone on the top of a Dartmoor tor, particularly on a dreary, misty day, and scan the far horizons, you will begin to appreciate that this is a unique environment. Despite a first impression of barren wasteland, here is an ancient landscape that has witnessed many events, both mundane and extraordinary. It is therefore steeped in a wealth of folklore, legends and ghost stories, some based on fact, others passed via word of mouth by people who have lived and worked here for generations.

This little book is a compilation of the genuinely bizarre and ghostly stories known on Dartmoor. It is intended to both entertain and inform you about some of the many strange tales Dartmoor has thrown up through the murky mists of time. If you believed every tale, you would probably never set foot there again because, as will be revealed, Dartmoor must have more ghosts than people living on it. If you throw in the Devil, headless horses, talking rivers, pigs that wear wigs, phantom cottages, and many more weird and wonderful tales, you have the makings of a truly sinister and supernatural place!

Dartmoor Bridge

- WHEN IS A GHOST NOT A GHOST? -

The solution to this riddle can be answered quite simply if the scene is a Dartmoor bog in the late evening or twilight. If you see a pale bluish flame flickering evanescently, then this is (probably) no spirit intent on luring you to a marshy demise. 'Ignis fatuus' – 'the foolish fire' or 'will-o'-the-wisp' is a natural phenomenon that occasionally appears over marshes. When viewed from a distance, it is easy to see how it may perpetuate strange stories.

- WELL I BE BOGGERED! -

This story, a favourite tale told by a former senior Dartmoor National Park officer, centres on the infamous depths of a Dartmoor mire. A young man was wending his way home across the moor, on foot, when he came across a valley bog with very treacherous parts – the locals call them 'feather beds' or 'quakers'. The young man espied a rather fine top hat resting delicately on the mire; unable to resist the temptation, he picked it up – only to find that beneath it was a man's head. The immersed gentleman smiled and introduced himself very politely; the moorman immediately offered to assist him out of his obvious predicament. His offer of help was accepted – but only on condition that the young man also rescued the horse on which the gentleman was seated!

- THE GREAT GRIMPEN MIRE -

Whilst on the subject of bogs, the famous Great Grimpen Mire was based on Foxtor Mires. Sir Arthur Conan Doyle used his fertile imagination to turn a local legend into a powerful drama, based around this and other locations. His Dartmoor-based story, *The Hound of the Baskervilles*, has been dramatized on numerous occasions, with several television and film versions actually being filmed on the moor. Conan Doyle regularly used to visit Bertram Fletcher Robinson, a friend who lived at Parke House, Ipplepen in Devon. On one of his outings, he visited the Royal Duchy Hotel at Princetown (which at one time became the prison officers' mess but is now a visitors' centre). Here he heard the story of a notorious character called Squire Cabell. This evil person, scared the local populace so much, that after his death in 1677, his coffin was secured by an enormous slab to make sure he didn't get out again! His casket was further entombed within a small building at Buckfastleigh.

Cabell had been a huntsman who, according to legend, sold his soul to the Devil. It is rumoured that phantom black hounds came to howl around his burial chamber. Presumably all the precautions against him came to naught, as stories are told of his ghostly hunt being heard in full cry. This made excellent literary fodder for turning into a first-rate story although, as in all good stories, the names of actual people and places have been changed to protect the 'innocent'. When it came to the choice of a suitably grand and impressive name for the ill-fated family, Conan Doyle demonstrated his tongue-in-cheek sense of humour, by using the name of the man who drove him to Princetown in his pony trap!

Buckfastleigh Church

- CHILDE THE HUNTER -

This Dartmoor legend is a traditional tale of sheer stupidity and out and out greed. Childe was a bachelor, the last of a long family line of well-to-do country folk. As he had no heirs, he inserted into his will a clause stating whichever church should bury him, would then possess all his lands. Then, duly endowed with death assurance, Childe went out onto the moor to hunt, in the depths of a snowy winter. Somehow, he was separated from the hunting party and became hopelessly lost on the southern moor, about four miles to the south of Princetown.

The flurry of snow, which had drifted large flakes down onto the moor all day, turned into a full-scale blizzard. At this point, Childe made a fatal mistake, his judgement perhaps impaired by the numbing cold. He cut off his lifeline, his horse, by killing and disembowelling it, then climbed inside its carcass for shelter and warmth. His final act was to leave a message in the snow, written in blood (there was probably a great deal of it around from his dead horse), reiterating his wishes.

It continued to snow for days afterwards and his frozen corpse lay out on the wasteland until a traveller chanced upon it. Presumably his message was still legible as this gentleman, who was bound north-westwards, spread the news of Childe's death and last request. As soon as the friars at Tavistock and the monks of Childe's native Plymstock got to hear the news, the race was on to fulfil the demands of his will. The friars of Tavistock reached the body first and made haste back to their town, but the monks lay in wait at the bridge where they expected the friars to cross the River Tavy. Tavistock's friars learned of the monks' plan and cleverly erected a pontoon over the river, at a spot which became known as Guile Bridge. They then managed to inter the body safely and claim their entitlement.

- BOWERMAN'S NOSE -

On the northern slopes of Hayne Down, about a mile from Hound Tor, is a strange rock idol called Bowerman's Nose, an enormous granite stack with a human-like shape. It is a natural formation, but at one time it was believed to be man-made or, more accurately, magically formed.

According to ancient tradition, this pile of rock was actually a brave, but foolish, giant called Bowerman. Bowerman was a hunter, who scoured the moors with his powerful pack of hounds. Although a strong man, he was a genial, cheerful chap and was much loved by the moorland community. However, in the days when he lived, the local witch population was large and very active in their dark pursuits. One day, a fateful confrontation occurred between the witches and Bowerman.

Hot in pursuit of his quarry, Bowerman had driven his pack through the coven; they were so outraged at the disruption he caused, that they vowed to wreak their revenge. Even Bowerman, so mighty and powerful, did not have the wit, guile or strength to avoid the ambush that the wicked witches set to ensnare him. One of the old hags turned herself into a hare and set off across the moors. She went over hill and dale pursued by the rapidly tiring hounds and hunter until, just as Bowerman thought that he had cornered the hare, he rode headlong into a trap. With venomous intent, the witches heaped a combined spell onto him, turning both him and his pack to stone. The great rock of Bowerman's Nose is said to be the giant himself, and the boulders strewn across the hillside are his hounds, petrified for eternity.

The great rock of Bowerman's Nose

- THE HOUNDS OF THE DEVIL -

The most famous hunter of all has to be the Devil. Not for him the mundane quarry of an ordinary fox or deer; he hunts for the souls of unbaptised babies. If anyone gazes on him or on his pack of spectral hounds, they will meet with certain death within a year. It is easy to identify this particular hunting pack, as it usually sets off at midnight from Wistman's Wood, half a mile north of Two Bridges. The Devil rides a headless black horse and the black hounds, known as the Wisht Hounds, with scorching laser-like red eyes, do his bidding. It is not uncommon to hear their baying, sometimes quite close by, as they invisibly range across the moor. They chase their victims towards the Dewerstone, driving them over the precipice of this near vertical rock face that is high above the River Plym. Some people say this is where the Devil lives on Dartmoor, with 'Dewer' being another name for the Devil.

- WHEN THE DEVIL HOLDS THE
TRUMP CARD... -

A part from being a keen huntsman, the Devil is also happy to participate in a spot of trading, but the interest rates are astronomical. One night, Jan Reynolds, a tin miner of bad character, paid the price of selling his soul to the Devil. It was 21 October 1638 when, on his way to collect his dues, the Devil called at the Tavistock Inn at Poundsgate to quaff some ale and get directions for Widecombe. He downed the brew, which sizzled and steamed as it washed down his throat after which he paid the landlady with a gold coin. The landlady's glee at the visitor's generosity diminished rather as, after he had left, the coin turned into a leaf and withered away.

Meanwhile, back at Widecombe-in-the-Moor, in the Church of St Pancras, the unsuspecting Jan Reynolds snoozed as the sermon wore on. In his hand he clutched a pack of cards. Suddenly the Devil turned on a spectacular natural firework display; a storm of high drama where exploding claps of thunder and enormous bolts of lightning flashed across the sky. Tethering his horse to one of the pinnacles, he burst into the church, seized Jan Reynolds and carried him away.

He rode northwards, climbing ever higher into the sky. Not far from the Warren House Inn, four of Jan's cards fell to the ground and formed the small fields known as The Devil's Playing Cards, the shape of each being recognizable as a different suit of cards. Later that night, the church itself was struck, with four people killed and many more badly injured by falling masonry. The story of this disaster is told in detail on the walls of the church.

The Church of St Pancras

- BRENTOR – SAINT MICHAEL
OF THE ROCK -

Having been deemed responsible for the near destruction of one church, the Devil has also been accused of trying to destroy another one before it was even built. This tale relates to the Church of St Michael of the Rock, on the volcanic, triangular hill of Brentor.

In 1884, the Revd Sabine Baring-Gould told how the Devil did his utmost to prevent the building of the church at this location, by regularly stealing the foundation stones. An Archangel knew of this and took a dim view; he hid himself behind Cox Tor, a mass of rocks five miles to the southeast and waited for the Devil. When the Devil arrived to vandalise the builders' efforts, the Archangel threw a huge rock at him. The stone, having travelled a long distance, hit the Devil between the horns and left him with a tremendous headache. As a result, the devil gave up his stealing and the church was built.

As with all stories of this type, there are variations. Another legend says that it was built by a sailor who survived a terrible storm and in gratitude, chose the first piece of land he spotted on reaching safety. However, the location of Brentor makes this a most unlikely possibility! It has to be one of the most distinctive landmarks in south-west England, as it can be seen from so many places on Dartmoor, the Plymouth area and east Cornwall. Perhaps it can even be seen from outer space, as this high hill has acquired a reputation as a spot frequently visited by UFOs.

The Church of St Michael of the Rock

- BRANSCOMBE'S LOAF & CHEESE -

There is a small granite-capped hill, high on Sourton Common and close to Meldon Reservoir, called Branscombe's Loaf. By chance, or a 'slice' of good luck, it has a lovely little story to explain its origin.

In the late thirteenth century, Walter Bronescombe, or Branscombe, was Bishop of Exeter. His diocese stretched across the length and breadth of Devon and Cornwall and, from time to time, he had to travel around the area. Now, on one particular occasion, whilst accompanied by his chaplain, he strayed from the King Way, the original road from Okehampton to Tavistock, and became lost in the mist. As the time passed by and the mist persisted, the Bishop and his chaplain developed hunger pangs. As one is wont to say in these circumstances, they declared they "would give anything for a bite to eat".

Miraculously, a stranger materialised out of the mist and approached them. He was an old man, with a skeletal face and frame, and he produced some bread and cheese. The Bishop was just about to accept this kind offering, when the chaplain let out a warning yell. He had spotted that the moorman's foot was cloven: absolute proof that it was the Evil One himself, confronting them. The uneaten bread and cheese dropped to the ground, and immediately turned into the rocks of that name today. The mist duly lifted and the Bishop and his chaplain went on their way, none the worse for wear, albeit with rumbling tummies, but infinitely grateful that they hadn't been obliged to pay the ultimate price for the devilish waiter service.

- CUTTY DYER -

The ancient stannary and borderland town of Ashburton possesses its own evil little sprite who appears in the shape of Cutty Dyer. He is easy to find as he lives near King's Bridge in the centre of the town. For many generations, naughty children who didn't mend their ways were threatened with a visit from him. However, misbehaving children were not his sole clients – he was particularly active against those folk who drank too much. He would eagerly waylay anyone in a state of alcoholic stupor as they staggered home. At best they could expect to be thrown into the River Ashburn, but at worst this evil little sprite would cut their throats, drink their blood and then throw them into the river! In the Middle Ages, an image or statue of St Christopher, patron saint of travellers, stood beside the river to help travellers when the Ashburn was in flood. Possibly a drunken reveller destroyed it, which turned the image into this large, red-eyed water sprite – 'Cutty' being a derivative of St Christopher and a 'Dyer' is defined as a scoundrel of the deepest dye – so beware!

- JAN COO -

The Ashburn is not the only Dartmoor river with a penchant for taking human life. The River Dart, which starts as two distinct flows, the East Dart and the West Dart, and then unites at Dartmeet to form the Dart, has acquired a cruel reputation.

The Dart flows with great power beneath towering hills before leaving Dartmoor at Buckfast. When it is considered just how many people use the river for recreational purposes, it is statistically likely that the river's reputation will live on. Jan Coo was a young orphan lad who lived at Rowbrook, just below Dartmeet. One night the boy heard a voice calling his name from the direction of the Dart. Although other workers on the farm could also hear the voice, Jan was convinced it was his name being called. This happened every evening until his curiosity got the better of him. No doubt you're thinking that with a name like Jan Coo there is a high possibility that local pigeons or cuckoos might well have been innocently calling out 'Coo Coo'. The story tells that young Jan ran off towards the river, and was never heard of or seen again...although neither was the eerie voice.

River Dart

- CRAZYWELL POOL -

Situated between Sheepstor and Princetown, Crazywell Pool is also renowned for calling out names; it is also endowed with an extremely apt name for a place associated with some strange and bizarre tales.

Crazywell Pool is in the parish of Walkhampton although it is actually quite a distance from that village. Locals would always be careful to avoid walking within earshot of the pool, as it is said that at dusk the pool calls out the name of the next person in the parish to die. Similarly, a quick visit to the pool at midnight on the eve of Midsummer's Day would show you the face of the next person to die reflected in the pond. We should imagine that to test this one out is a little chancy, as the odds must be that you will see your own reflection!

Two young lads who had been drinking in a local inn and scoffed at the tale decided to disprove it, with tragic results. They rode their motorcycles along the rough track that rises up from Burrator Reservoir and passes close to the pool. What happened that night will remain a mystery, as they were both killed while riding home. It is not a natural lake but an old tin mine, which has filled with water and is reputed to be bottomless. This inaccurate theory is based on the story that at one time all the bell ropes of Walkhampton Church were tied together and still failed to reach the bottom. It is unknown wether the bells were left on the end of the ropes to weigh them down, but as current thinking estimates the pool at a mere 15 feet deep, it seems likely that the ropes were quietly coiling up on the bottom!

- CRANMERE BENJI -

Whilst on a watery theme, let's consider Cranmere Pool. Actually, it is hardly worthy of such a title as even after heavy rain, it is little more than an overgrown puddle! It was once regarded as the most remote spot on the moors. Set high on a tableland of morass and mire, it remains a wild location today, although it is just about possible to drive a 4x4 within a mile of it via the looping, but gradually deteriorating, Artillery Road which almost encompasses it. To stand at Cranmere Pool, even today, is to be at a desolate spot, where the wind whistles incessantly and little sign of life will be seen.

With all its natural disadvantages, this spot became the location of the first 'letterbox' on Dartmoor. In 1854, James Perrot, the celebrated Chagford guide, left a bottle here so that the rare few visitors, each season, could leave their calling cards for others to peruse. Later, postcards were left, and the number of visitors recorded in the Visitors' Book grew greatly as the years passed. Perrot would probably be immensely proud if he knew how his solitary 'box' has become just one of literally thousands hidden on the moor.

One character who knew Cranmere, even before Perrot, was a gentleman called Benjamin Geyer, or Gear (also more familiarly Bingie, Binjy or Benji) from Okehampton. He was a trader who ran into hard times when several ships laden with his goods were captured by Turkish pirates. Left in a desperate plight, he hit on a salvage plan to protect his lifestyle. Without permission, he 'borrowed' or appropriated, some funds, maintained by public subscription and administered by himself as Mayor of Okehampton. However, he was wracked with guilt over his crime, and died in so troubled a state of mind that his spirit would not rest. Each night he could be heard in Okehampton, weeping and wailing.

The residents of the town became very upset by the nocturnal noises – even though they were harmless – and they called in a priest to rid them of their vociferous ghost. Alas, the priest was turned into a black colt, before a rider jumped onto his back and rode him at a mighty pace up on to the moor to Cranmere Pool. As they approached the pool, the rider jumped off, allowing the black colt to disappear, in spectacular fashion, beneath the waves never to be heard sobbing again. Until, of course, he appears in another version of the story...

Benjamin Gayer, Mayor of Okehampton on five occasions, was hanged after being convicted of sheep stealing. His soul was condemned to empty Cranmere Pool with a sieve. However, being a resourceful individual, and well versed in sheep stealing, he killed another sheep and lined the sieve with the sheepskin. He then easily emptied the pool, so successfully in fact that the waters of the pool cascaded down onto Okehampton, flooding the town. For this atrocious act, he was further sentenced to spin into ropes the sand in the bed of the now dry Cranmere Pool. This task still employs him, and he moans about it on stormy nights, growling and wailing in protest.

- WIDECOMBE-IN-THE-MOOR -

We've already seen what the Devil did to Widecombe Church, but this small moorland village, made world-famous by a folk song about its Fair, has also been troubled by other ghosts. The Old Inn is haunted by a ghost called 'Harry' who, occasionally in mid-afternoon, walks from the kitchen into a room that has only solid stone walls and no exit, and disappears. He has been seen many times but, unlike the standard see-through, almost

Widecombe-in-the-Moor sign

21

wimpish apparition, Harry has a very solid, real look about him. He doesn't scare people because he is so lifelike. The sounds of a sobbing child have also been heard in an upstairs bedroom, within the same inn. Someone cries for endless hours, but when the door is opened, the tears subside and there is nobody there!

On his tours of the West Country, the Revd Sabine Baring-Gould unearthed many folk songs and ballads, but the one about Widecombe Fair is the best known. From the words of the song, we learn that "when the wind whistles cold on the moor of a night, Tom Pearce's grey mare doth appear ghostly white."

It would be hard to find an animal that had better cause to reappear as a ghost, than this poor creature. Just imagine the scene when seven hulking great country boys, living long ago in a band of countryside almost twenty long moorland miles to the north of Widecombe, all decided to have a day out at this fair. On the outward journey, they quite sensibly took turns to ride the old grey mare they had borrowed from Tom Pearce. But having sampled too much of the strong, heady cider on offer, were so drunk at the end of the day, that for the homeward journey they all clambered on board the poor old horse. Quite clearly the poor horse couldn't take the strain; she collapsed and died soon after leaving Widecombe. Now, from time to time, the rattlings of her bones are heard in the vicinity. The worthless characters who, with their drunken frolicking caused her premature demise, have all been named in the song, but the poor old grey mare remains anonymous.

- A FAIR WAY TO GO? -

In the early nineteenth century, fairs were mainly agricultural meets, and were important features on the moorman's calendar. Brent Fair was one such event not to be missed. A farmer, who lived at Round Hill, on the road from Two Bridges to Princetown, was determined to have a good day out and do a bit of business as well! Some versions of this sorry tale suggest that he sold his old horse for a song, got completely drunk and then bought back the same horse for a much higher amount; other versions just say he was cheated on a deal. Either way, he was obviously very unhappy with the outcome.

Meanwhile, waiting back at home, his wife heard the unmistakable sounds of his horse plodding into the stable. She waited a few minutes and then, as he did not appear, she lit a lantern and went out to see what was keeping him. Outside there was no sign of life: no horse and no husband. The bewildered lady had to wait until the following day to learn that it definitely could not have been her husband she heard returning home. He had hanged himself from a tree near Combestone Tor, at a point on the road from Holne to Hexworthy. This was about four miles short of home. After that, the place was always referred to as Hangman's Pit.

- A PHANTOM PIG & HER PIGLETS -

Dartmoor is noted for its sheep, cattle and ponies, which are a common sight, wandering freely over the moors. More worthy of a second glance, though, would be the sight of an old sow and her litter of hungry little piglets trotting across the moor. When the moors are misty and the day is decidedly dull and dreary, you could perhaps see such a scene. But these may be no ordinary little porky creatures... for there is a phantom family, destined to travel the same route from Merripit Hill (the high hill on the Moretonhampstead side of Postbridge) to Cator Gate, a venue in the central depression of Dartmoor. Usually on misty days, their journey of a few miles is undertaken because they are hungry and have heard of the body of a dead horse at Cator. With great enthusiasm and anticipation, they descend to Cator, only to find that the horse has already been eaten. A pathetic scene follows as the little piglets wail and squeal 'Skin and Bones, Skin and Bones' as they disconsolately start their return journey to Merripit Hill. As they downheartedly trot along, they become increasingly hungry. Their plight is so acute that they end up emaciated and the cycle of hope and despair is re-enacted over and over.

- JUDGE JEFFREYS & THE BIG BLACK
PHANTOM PIG -

But not all ghostly pigs deserve quite so much sympathy! George Jeffreys, the First Baron Jeffreys, was the English judge who became notorious for his harsh sentencing at the Bloody Assizes after the Monmouth Rebellion in 1685. His severe sentencing, for even minor indiscretions, earned him a black reputation. In his travels as a judge on the Western Circuit, he held court in many Devonshire towns and legend suggests he was at his judicial best (or worst) at Lydford. Although there is no solid evidence of the judge ever having been to Lydford, he must have had a great impact on the area as, so the story goes, he haunts the ancient borough in the guise of a big black pig! It is not clear how often this phantom porker has been seen, or why indeed it should automatically be assumed it was the dreadful judge himself as, he is also supposed to haunt a room in a hotel in Exeter. However, at least in Exeter he is in a more recognizable human form! Whether or not it is him, or indeed if he haunts anywhere, you will have to 'judge' for yourself.

- THE WHITE BIRD OF OXENHAM -

South Zeal is a small village located on the northern side of Dartmoor. It lies between the A30 and the towering Cosdon or Cawsand Hill, and is the scene of one of Dartmoor's strangest sequences of events. There is a lovely old stone pub called the Oxenham Arms, which derived its name from a local family whose history dated back to Elizabeth I. Oxenham Manor, their family home, is about one mile to the north-east of South Zeal, as close to the boundary of the Dartmoor National Park as you could get. The Oxenham family were haunted by the apparition of a white-breasted bird; if a family member saw it, death followed almost immediately. Admittedly some of the Oxenhams who died were already on their deathbeds when the white bird fluttered over them, but there were also sightings by healthy members who met with untimely deaths.

Lady Margaret Oxenham had a visitation on the eve of her wedding. Her father saw it fluttering over her head but said nothing. Perhaps if he had, she might have been warned to be careful, for on the following day, at the wedding ceremony, a jealous ex-lover rushed into South Tawton Church and plunged a knife into Margaret's back; he then pulled it out and killed himself.

It should be pointed out that it was not just the fevered imagination of a dying person who saw the bird each time; many respectable witnesses, in full control of their faculties, would all swear to having seen the bird. During the eighteenth century, William Oxenham was feeling slightly off colour when the bird was sighted over him. He boldly proclaimed that he might be sick, but he certainly wasn't that sick. Within three days, he was dead and buried. The white bird followed the family around until the last of this Oxenham line passed away in Canada in the twentieth century. Unfortunately, no-one noticed whether the bird hopped over the Atlantic, then decided to stay in Canada, or whether in fact it never saw off its last victim. It is known though, that the death of his father, in Exeter, was preceded by a visit from a white bird. There are, of course, many pigeons around the city centre, but even if one had accidentally found its way into the death chamber...it would certainly have been an odd coincidence!

- LADY HOWARD -

There is no telling what sort of sentence Judge Jeffreys might have inflicted on Lady Howard who, according to the folklore story, supposedly murdered her four husbands.

This story has developed as a result of mistaken identity, as the deeds of one Lady Frances Howard have been attributed to another – Lady Mary Howard. Perhaps this is why her ghost is such a bizarre manifestation. If you see her, then take some consolation in the fact that her only real crime was to cut off her children's inheritance. Nevertheless, she is doomed to a never-ending chore. She has to visit Okehampton Castle every night to pluck a single blade of grass.

Okehampton Castle

The castle was part of the Fitzford Estates; she was the granddaughter of Sir John Fitz of Fitzford near Tavistock. It is her ghoulish means of transport to the castle, and the nature of the journey, that is so remarkable, even for a legend. Lady Howard becomes a big black dog. She runs beside a coach or carriage, which is constructed from the bones of the four husbands she is alleged to have murdered. If you throw in four headless horses and a headless coachman, you are left with quite a bizarre spectacle.

The whole entourage has to travel from Fitzford near Tavistock to Okehampton and back. Unusual as her mode of transport may be, she is indeed very fortunate that she doesn't have to rely on public transport on this route. She doesn't use the A386 because it didn't exist in the days when she began her sorties into the night. Instead, she uses the original route, which scales the heights of the moor, one can only imagine the awful weather she must encounter at times when she embarks on her nightly quest. Occasionally she has been spotted just off the route. At Bridestowe she has been seen at The Royal Oak and also at the Ghost Tree, which after all, has to be the ideal spot for a ghost dog.

- HIS MASTER'S VENGEANCE -

Another black dog is to be found on the road from Princetown to Plymouth. Local legend says that he was the pet of a traveller murdered many years ago, who travels the lonely road looking for the murderer of his master so he may take his revenge. Unfortunately, he has been known to make mistakes. Many years ago, a visitor was walking along in winter when he was joined by the companionable animal. Fond of dogs, he tried to pat its head, but was suitably alarmed when his hand passed right through it. Suddenly, a flash of lightning struck him, and he wasn't found until the next day – still unconscious – but obviously lucky to be alive.

- THE DOG-GONED PONSWORTHY PIG -

Yet another black dog was found near Ponsworthy, by a local man who just happened to be on his way back from the pub at Hexworthy. He tied his scarf around the dog's neck and led him home, locking him in his stable for the night. The following morning, when he invited his neighbours to inspect his captive, he was embarrassed to find his scarf tied around the neck of a large black pig! It is clearly possible that the spirit in this story owes more to the Forest Inn at Hexworthy than to the spirit world!

- SQUIRE FULFORD -

Lady Howard's coach is not the only one on Dartmoor to be pulled by headless horses. There is a haunted house, called Great Fulford, on the eastern side of Dartmoor. One of the old Squire Fulford's coaches has occasionally been seen near Dunsford, driven along the lanes by the old cavalier gentleman himself. This phantom coach is pulled by four headless horses, but, unfortunately, history doesn't tell us the reason for the Squire's outings.

- THUNDERING HOOVES & HEADLESS HORSES -

Several decades ago, a young man proudly took his friends off on a jaunt across the moors in his new car. As they reached high ground, they became enveloped by a thick mist and they soon mistook the line of the road and drifted onto open moorland. They immediately realised their mistake, but the mist was so dense they could not see the road at all. As in all good ghost stories, instead of staying in the safety of the car, they got out to look for the road.

Suddenly, to their great astonishment, they heard the sound of thundering hooves quickly bearing down on them. As they gazed into the mist, they were transfixed by the ghostly sight of several headless horses – all mounted by headless riders – encircling them, menacingly. Fearing for their lives, they cranked the engine, dropping the starting handle in their panic. Frantically, they drove away, finally regaining the road after a bit of bumping and skidding. A day or so later, when the conditions were a little better, the young man decided to go back for his starting handle. He located the spot and retrieved the lost tool. Embedded in the ground, he saw not only the footprints of himself and his friends, plus the tyre marks of his car, but also the hoofprints of galloping and stomping horses. But they did not lead away from, or up to, the spot!

A similar event occurred when the Chagford Home Guard were on duty at Gidleigh, one night in 1943. On a clear bright, moonlit night, the sound of galloping hooves raced up to and passed them, but no horses were seen.

- THE GHOST TOR RIDER -

Between Powder Mills and Two Bridges, the B3212 passes below an eminent pile of rocks called Crockern Tor. This point is close to the centre of Dartmoor and was used, from 1305 to 1749, for open air meetings of the Tinners' or Stannary Parliament (Stannum is Latin for tin). The tor was chosen because it was about an equal distance for the twenty-four representatives who were sent from each of the four Stannary towns, situated in each corner or 'quarter' of the moor. They might well have had an uninvited member joining them at their twice-yearly meetings for 'Old Crockern' favoured dark nights for his adventures across Dartmoor. This mysterious horseman had a skeleton steed and was a truly frightening sight to behold. It is believed that he might well have been associated with the Wisht Hounds, as their 'kennel' in Wistman's Wood lies just over the hill from Crockern Tor. Nobody knows who this mysterious rider is, or why he haunts this tor and surrounding moor.

Crockern Tor

- A SILVER-HAIRED RIDER -

The road from Haytor towards Widecombe is much used by visitors to eastern Dartmoor. There is a stretch of it which curves and twists below Rippon Tor and leads, in a short while, to the crossroads at Hemsworthy Gate. From time to time, a phantom rider has been known to speed along here; he can be identified by his distinctive silver hair and an old-fashioned military style mackintosh. There is not a lot of point in following him, as you can be sure that by the time Hemsworthy Gate is reached, he will have dissolved into thin air! Other reports have indicated that a phantom coach (of the coach and horses variety) also clatters along this stretch.

- THE A38 GHOSTS -

The A38 Exeter to Plymouth road skirts the southern edge of Dartmoor and passes by old Dartmoor towns and villages such as Ashburton, Buckfastleigh, South Brent and Ivybridge. Today's road is a fast highway, which happens to be haunted by a hitchhiking ghost. However, in the past, the route between Devon's premier settlements was a much quieter coaching road, except of course when the midnight coach thundered through the night during the 1830s and '40s. This coach has travelled along the old road at various times since then but, although the unmistakable sounds of horses' hooves and rattling wheels can be clearly heard, the coach is never seen. Perhaps this is why the phantom hitchhiker never uses it.

- THE HAIRY HANDS -

Of the many stories that abound on Dartmoor, this is the one of which most people have heard, possibly because the B3212 road between Postbridge and Two Bridges (or between the East and West Dart River) is very well-travelled. Anyone who already knows the tale will make quite sure that their fellow travellers also learn the story!

Shortly after 1910, a series of strange incidents occurred along this route. Most of them happened near a farm called Archerton near Postbridge. Cyclists felt their handlebars wrenched out of their hands, forcing them off the road; pony traps were put out of control and ended up in the ditch beside the road. Later, cars and motor coaches suffered similar fates, sometimes with fatal results.

Dr Helby, a local man from Princetown, was riding his motorbike and sidecar, when it inexplicably veered out of control. Two children, passengers in the sidecar, were thrown out and survived but the doctor was killed. Shortly afterwards, an Army officer riding his motorcycle along this stretch, was badly injured but survived to reveal that a pair of large, muscular hairy hands closed over his own and forced him off the road. This revelation led to sensational frontpage headlines. The Daily Mail sent reporters to investigate the story with their reports resulting in a full-scale enquiry by various authorities into the state of the road.

It was always possible that an adverse camber could have caused problems, so repairs were carried out to the road surface. But that wouldn't explain why, one night in the mid-1920s, a lady in a caravan parked by the side of this road, saw a large hairy hand clawing its way up the outside of the window. In sheer panic, she made a sign of the cross and the hairy hand disappeared, never to be seen by her again.

Between 1910 and 1930 there was a number of serious incidents, but since those times the strange occurrences, which have undoubtedly happened along that road, have not been as dramatic. There was at least one fatal accident involving an overturned car, but as the young occupant was found dead at the scene, we will never know whether the hairy hands played a murderous role, or whether it was simply an accident. Nevertheless, many people will feel a sense of unease, particularly between the Cherry Brook Bridge and Postbridge, and keep a wary eye out for any hairy intruders.

It is not only this stretch of the B3212 that is haunted. Just over a mile to the north-east of the Warren House Inn is a spot where the road roller-coasters down into a hollow before rising again. This tiny stream, at the head of Green Combe, is the East Bovey River. It is not clear whether or not it is the sudden sharp drop into this deep hollow that is the cause, but several people (and dogs) have experienced sudden cold and been overcome with great fear at this spot. Cyclists have complained that they have felt their bicycles enduring such great stresses that they thought the bikes were about to fall apart, only to be perfectly all right again on the ascending opposite side of the depression.

- THE WATCHING PLACE -

About four miles from Moretonhampstead, on the B3212 road over Dartmoor, is a mysterious and sinister spot called the Watching Place. It is located where the road is met by the B3344, which wends its way from the Manaton direction. Its name appears on the signpost, but its origin is worthy of some consideration. It is believed that the local Lord of the Manor once possessed the right to have gallows on the edge of his lands. This particular gallows at the Watching Place was far from redundant, with a large proportion of its 'clients' being drawn from the highwaymen trade, some of these individuals left to dangle long after their death, as an example to any others contemplating similar exploits.

The Watching Place was thus where relatives or friends had to wait and watch before being allowed to remove their dead. Alternatively, it has been suggested that the Watching Place is where the highwaymen actually watched out for their intended victims. Whoever was watching, it has been known for animals, ridden, led or driven, to react strongly to passing this point, experiencing perhaps, a feeling of being watched?

- THE WARREN HOUSE -

The Warren House is a remote inn on the Moreton to Postbridge road. A few centuries ago, the original inn stood on the opposite side of the road to the present one, and the innkeeper and his family would have led an extremely isolated existence. The bulk of their custom would have come from the tin miners, who worked the many mines in the vicinity of the inn.

An amusing story that has been passed around for many years, tells of how, at the end of a spell of wintry weather, when the moors had been covered in snow for weeks, a visitor called at the inn in search of overnight accommodation. He was shown to his room, in which was a large chest. The visitor stared at it for

ages wondering what treasures it might contain until, eventually, his curiosity got the better of him. As he lifted the heavy lid, he had the shock of his life; inside was a corpse with an extremely white, ghostly face. Thinking he had uncovered a murder victim, he ran downstairs screaming. Almost nonchalantly, the landlord said, "Don't worry, tiz only feyther." 'Father' had died a few weeks earlier; his corpse had been salted down to preserve it until the weather relented, and it could be carried for burial at the parish church many miles away across the moor.

There is, however, another story, which may well be construed as murder. Two men in the inn had an argument over their drinks, and one threatened the other. A few nights later, unseen by his victim, he drew a 'magic circle' in chalk around the man's feet. Sure enough, within a short time, his opponent took ill and passed away.

- EPHRAIM'S PINCH -

Soussons is a huge coniferous forest that can be seen sprawling over the low hills to the south of the B3212 near the Warren House. Trees cover most of the small hill, called Ephraim's Pinch, on the south side of this forest. The name is derived from an old story about a young man who had to show his would-be father-in-law that he had sufficient strength and fortitude to be worthy as a suitor to for his daughter. The task was set. Ephraim had to carry a bag of wheat six miles from Widecombe to Runnage, a farm in the vicinity of Soussons, have it ground and then carry it back without once putting it down for a rest. Ephraim was so determined not to fail, that he strained himself badly and died from his injuries. The little hill where he collapsed is thus named in honour of his gallant, or foolish, attempt to win the hand of his loved one.

- PRINCETOWN'S PHANTOMS -

To most people 'Dartmoor' is the prison and it is this grim edifice that springs to mind whenever its name is mentioned. Initially, this place of confinement was set up as a prisoner of war depot to accommodate thousands of French prisoners, and later, in 1812, many Americans. In 1850, it became a convict prison. Throughout its years, many men have died there.

David Davies was sent there in 1879; over two terms of almost consecutive imprisonment, he spent a total of 50 years at Princetown until his death in 1929. For a large part of the duration of his stay, he was entrusted to be a shepherd on the open moor, a job that he fell in love with and refused to give up. On his release from his first term of imprisonment, he begged to stay on in the same capacity, but this was refused. As a result, and on his release, Davies committed a crime, and was sentenced to return to his beloved post. At lambing time, David was allowed to stay out on the moors tending to his flock.

The dedication of this man to his task was so considerable that, after he died, it is said he returned to the moor that he knew and loved so much. Many is the foggy night when the spectral shape of this spirit shepherd can be seen fleeting amongst the bleating sheep. His grey outline is a shy one that disappears within seconds of being seen by any human: it is for his sheep that he haunts his old territory.

Princetown is supposedly the highest town in England, and the Plume of Feathers is the oldest building in the town. It was built in 1785, many years before the prison. Not surprisingly, such a wonderful old building has had its moments. The original ladies' toilet, on the eastern side of the building, has been known to cause a few scares. On many occasions, a sudden icy presence was felt; the effect was so scary that some ladies ran out. No historical reason is known for this. Meanwhile, in a middle room upstairs, several guests complained that, whilst they have slumbered in their beds, they have had to hold onto their sheets whilst some invisible force tried to tug them off. It is believed that long ago the sound of a mother sobbing

Princetown

Dartmoor Prison illustration

37

was frequently heard, crying over the death of her child. A previous landlord did not believe in ghosts, but admitted that one night, whilst asleep in the top floor room, he was awoken by the unmistakable sounds of footsteps: they walked right across the bedroom and back again. The resident Labrador dogs would not go near this room: perhaps aware of an unnatural presence?

Since the building was re-roofed in 1983, none of these particular experiences have recurred. However, early one morning a lady, dressed in a brown cloak, walked the entire length of the inn. On inspection, nobody could be found there ... which is strange because there are no other exits and the building is solidly constructed. The witness of this was not immediately afraid of the passing person because she looked so real but, on realization of what had happened, was shaken for several days after the event.

Another obvious venue in Princetown for ghosts is the cemetery where many French and American prisoners of war are buried. They endured often harsh conditions at Princetown and the number of untimely deaths has led to many sightings of ghosts at this spot. Although there was a gap of almost forty years between the war depot closing and the convict prison opening, the two completely separate establishments are linked by one unusual ghost story.

An old-timer, serving a sentence for deception, had managed to convince the authorities that he could be trusted to work outside the prison. But temptation overcame him and one misty day, when nobody was looking, he slipped away from his working party. Within hours he began to regret the folly of his actions as the Dartmoor mist had made him lose his sense of direction. Ill-equipped for such a foolish venture, the old con lost his confidence and began to despair. Suddenly, out of the mist, loomed two marching figures dressed in early nineteenth century uniforms. Not stopping to question their presence on the moor, the convict hurriedly set off after them. In total silence, they marched through the gloom, until they walked straight into the lights of the search party out looking for the escapee. Seconds later, the two accompanying soldiers completely vanished into thin air. It is believed that these two men, from more than a century earlier, were part of a trio who perished on the moor in a blizzard. It has been calculated that the spot where the convict encountered them, was probably the spot where two of them died. If you are ever out on the moor, make sure you have a map and compass – it's far more reliable than waiting to be rescued by a ghost.

- LEGIONS OF GHOSTS -

Although the Romans paid little attention to Dartmoor, it is rumoured that the ancient camp on Hunter's Tor, above Lustleigh Cleave, was of Roman origin. This notion has been created because, when the moon is full, Roman legionnaires have been seen at this spot. It seems that their spirits are condemned to fight a never-ending battle. The Cleave is one of the loveliest, most wooded valleys on the moor. But take care if you happen to hear the sound of the hunt – it may not be quite what you think, but another ghostly gathering. This hunting party is centuries old; locals who have seen it describe the riders travelling through the valley as being dressed in Tudor garments. However, there have also been many other occasions when they have been heard without being seen. On these occasions, one wonders how it is known that this is the Tudor pack.

- CHAGFORD'S CAVALIER GHOST -

In a Civil War skirmish, Sidney Godolphin, a young Cavalier, was mortally wounded by a musket shot. He died in the porch of what is now the Three Crowns Hotel in Chagford. But the story does not quite end there; visitors staying at the inn have seen the figure of a Cavalier in the hotel corridors. It walks along a landing and just keeps going. After one sighting, a visitor actually identified him as Sidney, from a painting hanging in the hotel.

The Teign, above Chagford, has a delightful tributary called the Blackaton Brook. On one of the small stone bridges that spans the stream in the vicinity of Gidleigh, the sound of hand to hand fighting between Cavaliers and Roundheads has frequently been heard during the night.

- CASTLES IN THE AIR? -

Chagford, the ancient stannary town on the north-eastern side of Dartmoor, has long been a favoured inland resort. For two Edwardian ladies used to the hustle and bustle of London, it was the ideal place to spend a quiet holiday in the country. The ladies were so intent on having a wonderful time, that they travelled down to Dartmoor for a brief stay to seek out the perfect place to rent. Leaving their Chagford hotel, they went for a stroll to look for their dream holiday home. On the outskirts of the town, they found it – a beautiful cottage with neat lawns, garlanded in roses. Hoping, perhaps even presuming, that it could be rented, they knocked on the door, whereupon a pretty little girl, dressed immaculately in white, invited them into a lovely, neat sitting room. The girl's mother was also dressed in white and was beautifully ornamented with expensive jewellery. A cat lay contentedly asleep on a hearth rug and yes, it too was completely white.

The visiting ladies felt slightly uncomfortable but enquired whether they could rent the cottage. The dates they wanted were not available, but they were so taken with the cottage that they agreed to change the date of their holiday so that they could have it. Arrangements made, they cheerfully returned to London. However, when the ladies came back down to Devon, they had the shock of their lives: the cottage of their dreams had turned into a nightmare. Faced with a bed of nettles strewn with rubble, it was clear that it had been demolished many years earlier.

- THE GHOST BRIDE OF CHAGFORD -

The grave of Mary Whiddon lies in Chagford churchyard. It was in October 1641, that she was cruelly shot down by a former lover as she walked up the aisle on her wedding day. It was this sorry tale which R.D. Blackmore adapted into his famous story of *Lorna Doone*, cleverly disguised by a change of moor from Dartmoor to Exmoor! Her family's estate was Whiddon Park, just over a mile from Chagford. In 1971, a daughter of the same house married at Chagford Church. One of the guests staying there for the event, awoke at dawn to see the outline of a young bride wearing a wedding dress, appropriate for the time of Mary Whiddon. The modern bride placed her bouquet on Mary's grave in a gesture of respect, care and consideration for a troubled and wronged spirit.

St Michael's Church, Chagford

- LANDLOCKED SAILORS -

Nearby is the Northmore Arms, one of the loveliest little pubs on the moor. Despite being as far from the sea as is possible in Devon, its ghost is that of an old bearded and bewhiskered sailor. He stands in the corner of the bar and has been seen by some of the locals – not necessarily after they have been drinking. Interestingly, the pub lies on an ancient route called The Mariners' Way, that ran from parts of North Devon (Bideford and Barnstaple) down to Dartmouth in South Devon. This old mariner, or sailor, must have had cause to visit this wayside inn. The route was well used by sailors changing ship; it saved having to sail all around Cornwall. If you are so disposed, you can even follow lengthy sections of this cross-country route yourself.

- ANYONE HOME? -

There is a maze of lanes between Bovey Tracey and Haytor, the sort of rural area that looks as if nothing ever happens to it. Millions of visitors, who pass close by on their way to Dartmoor, never give it a second look. Perhaps they should.

At various times from at least a century ago, until even quite recently, a strange phenomenon occurs. There have been several independent sightings, usually from people walking in the area, of a cottage, seen below on the lower hillsides, beside a wood on a narrow, rough track. The strange thing is, that no such cottage exists and people looking to locate it have been confounded by its nonexistence. Old maps confirm that no such cottage was ever there, but the hedge, in the vicinity, contains myrtle, which was a favoured hedging plant by locals, suggesting that there might well have been a cottage here once. To live in a phantom cottage like this would certainly deal with unwanted callers or the postman delivering bills.

- THE 9.15PM GHOSTS -

There is a fine line between a cottage that could be described as quaint, and one that is about to fall down. Millbrook Cottage at Moretonhampstead turned from the former into the latter.

The Milton family, who lived there during the Second World War, sensibly moved out before it fell down around their ears. Behind them, they left long rambling gardens, which were used by a local man in which to keep poultry. Now, although midnight is generally accepted as the 'witching hour' for 'ghoulies and ghosties, long legged beasties and things that go bump in the night', at this derelict cottage, a series of ghostly occurrences happened at precisely 9.15pm. The apparitions on each occasion were different: a silhouetted figure, seen against a moonlit snow scene, left no footprints and vanished into thin air. Another man visiting the cottage, at 9.15pm, was grabbed by the throat by an invisible force, before being dumped unceremoniously on the ground. A small boy apparently ran through an open doorway but, as the church clock of Moreton struck 9.15pm, the boy disappeared. There were many other disquieting events, which all coincided with this mid-evening maelstrom of mysterious manifestations.

- THE GOLDEN GHOST -

Dartmoor and the surrounding lands have always been difficult to farm and this was the case for the Collins family in the 1830s. Mary Collins laboured long and hard and managed to eke out an existence. But she could only work by day; every night she had to lock all the windows and bolt all the doors, in order to keep out the forbidding figure of a tall ghost who stalked the farmyard and its outbuildings.

One night her son had a fever and cried out for water, but the water was outside in a courtyard well. Bravely, Mary picked up a bright lantern and set off on her mission of mercy. As she drew the water from the well, the tall ghost appeared beside her. In a deep bass voice, he challenged her presence, to which Mary replied, "In the name of God, why do you trouble me?" The ghost gently led her to a location on the farm where he told her that she must dig in the ground at first light. This she did, and she came upon a crock of gold coins, which kept her and her family in relative comfort for the rest of their lives. The ghost was never seen again.

Dartmoor National Park

- JAY'S GRAVE -

Kitty Jay's wayside grave is sited on the road between Hound Tor and Heatree Cross. Solid facts are hard to establish about this young girl, who is believed to have committed suicide after becoming pregnant out of wedlock. In keeping with tradition, she had to be buried at the nearest crossroads, rather than in the consecrated ground of a parish church cemetery. Until 1823, the law required that suicides and criminals should be buried at a crossroads, with a stake through their bodies. The idea was that their troubled spirits would not be able to find their way back to the village. Who Kitty Jay really was is not known, for the story passed down through time has warped and distorted, although the 'bare bones' of the tale are probably close to the truth.

In 1860, James Bryant, a road mender, discovered bones in a rough grave; it was at first supposed they were that of an animal. When it was discovered they were those of a young woman, his wife had vaguely remembered a story told to her by her own mother about an orphan girl who hanged herself. The bones were re-buried in their present position and for many years fresh flowers appeared daily on her grave, creating their own mystery, as nobody knew who did this caring deed. It has been suggested by some that it was the pixies who left them; others say that Beatrice Chase, the eccentric novelist, was responsible.

Kitty Jay's story has been told so often that people consider it to be a sign of good luck to leave a small posy of moorland flowers on her grave. Her ghost has reputedly been seen hovering over the grave by people travelling past; although this is unsubstantiated, some folk will go on quite lengthy detours to avoid the spot. There are other suicide victims buried in similar circumstances at different locations on Dartmoor, the most notable being George Stephens, whose grave is on the high, open moor, a few miles from Peter Tavy. George fell in love, but the girl's father forbade her to see him. Sorely afflicted, the young man gorged himself on the leaves of highly poisonous belladonna (deadly nightshade) and soon died. His grave is much farther from any recognised road, being little more than a crossroads of paths.

Hound Tor

- TOM WHITE & THE PIXIES -

Dartmoor wouldn't be Dartmoor without its pixies – those mischievous little creatures who so densely populate the moor. Stories abound, but there is only room for one short one. There once lived a handsome young moorman called Tom White. He was fit and strong and thought nothing of walking four miles across Bellever Tor and down to Huccaby Farm on the West Dart River, to meet his sweetheart. One night, Tom left Huccaby and started home. Beyond Laughter Tor, he dropped to the East Dart River where he heard music nearby. He soon saw hundreds of tiny pixies having their own party, dancing and prancing and jumping about. Naturally, Tom was spotted and he was forced to dance with them; although he became weary, he simply could not stop until dawn. The pixies disappeared, leaving Tom in a state of complete exhaustion. He vowed never to go out on the moor at night again, a promise so seriously taken, that he forsook his young lady at Huccaby.

- VIXANA THE WITCH -

An appropriate story to end this book is that of Vixana, the ugliest old crone of a witch ever to darken the moors. The legendary Vixana had a face as wrinkled as a walnut, liberally spiced with a profusion of warts and spots. Her hair was like straggly straw, her teeth were green, black and festering and her nose was long and hooked. She was as evil as she was ugly, and this diabolical person made her home in a rockpile close to a major path across the moor on the Two Bridges to Tavistock Road. Beside it was a mire, so deep it would easily accommodate all who stepped in it.

Whenever a wayfarer passed close to Vixana's home, she would use her evil powers to conjure up a mist. Totally lost, the poor victim would eventually wander into the mire and be drawn into a vat of mud and ooze, whilst the wicked witch stood and gloated. Well, of course, the moor folk were not over enthusiastic about such goings on and were desperately keen to rid the moor of such an evil force. By a sheer stroke of good luck, there happened to be a handsome young moorman who had been awarded a magic ring as a result of services given to the pixies; whenever he put this ring on, he became invisible. And so, the moorman was employed to sort out the evil Vixana.

One day, as the moorman approached her tor, she spied him and immediately conjured up a mist, completely covering him. However, he kept his wits about him and put on his magic ring. He cleverly avoided the mire to reach the base of the tor – one of the highest granite piles on the moor. With his great strength and sure-footedness, he stealthily and silently climbed to the top of the tor, where the perplexed witch stood peering into the mist. As she dwelt on where the young man had gone, he rushed towards her and threw her over the cliff face. With no time to grab her broomstick, she crashed to a spectacular death.